SandCastle™
Baby Animals

Calves

Alex Kuskowski

A Division of ABDO

ABDO
Publishing Company

Consulting Editor, Diane Craig, M.A./Reading Specialist

visit us at www.abdopublishing.com

Published by ABDO Publishing Company, a division of ABDO, P.O. Box 398166, Minneapolis, Minnesota 55439. Copyright © 2014 by Abdo Consulting Group, Inc. International copyrights reserved in all countries. No part of this book may be reproduced in any form without written permission from the publisher. SandCastle™ is a trademark and logo of ABDO Publishing Company.

Printed in the United States of America, North Mankato, Minnesota
062013
012014

Editor: Liz Salzmann
Content Developer: Alex Kuskowski
Cover and Interior Design and Production: Mighty Media, Inc.
Photo Credits: Shutterstock, Thinkstock

Library of Congress Cataloging-in-Publication Data

Kuskowski, Alex.
  Calves / by Alex Kuskowski ; consulting editor, Diane Craig, M.A./reading specialist.
    pages cm -- (Baby animals)
  ISBN 978-1-61783-836-1
1. Calves--Juvenile literature. I. Title.
  SF205.K87 2014
  599.55'91392--dc23
                        2012049661

SandCastle™ Level: Beginning

SandCastle™ books are created by a team of professional educators, reading specialists, and content developers around five essential components—phonemic awareness, phonics, vocabulary, text comprehension, and fluency—to assist young readers as they develop reading skills and strategies and increase their general knowledge. All books are written, reviewed, and leveled for guided reading, early reading intervention, and Accelerated Reader® programs for use in shared, guided, and independent reading and writing activities to support a balanced approach to literacy instruction. The SandCastle™ series has four levels that correspond to early literacy development. The levels are provided to help teachers and parents select appropriate books for young readers.

Emerging Readers   Beginning Readers   Transitional Readers   Fluent Readers
   (no flags)   (1 flag)   (2 flags)   (3 flags)

Contents

Calves

A baby cow is a calf.
Calves are raised on
farms. They live in
barns and fields.

Most cows have one calf per year.

A newborn calf can stand right after it is born. It stays close to its mother.

Walter and Lucy are calves. Lucy rests in the grass. Cows **graze** for eight hours a day.

Jayden listens to his calf moo. Calves use noises to **communicate**.

Calves are playful and curious. These calves are **exploring** a field.

Kayla gives her calf Misty a snack. Misty is nine months old.

Did You Know?

▶ Most calves weigh 50 to 100 pounds (23 to 45 kg) when they are born.

▶ Calves are usually born in the spring.

▶ A calf's stomach has four **chambers**.

▶ Calves are raised in most countries around the world.

Calf Quiz

Read each sentence below. Then decide whether it is true or false.

1. Calves are raised on farms.

2. A newborn calf does not stay close to its mother.

3. Lucy does not rest in the grass.

4. Cows and calves live in herds.

5. Misty is one year old.

Glossary

chamber – an enclosed space or section.

communicate – to share ideas, information, or feelings.

explore – to learn about a place by walking all around it.

graze – to eat grass that is growing in a field.